To Julius,
from all your
friends at Thurrock.
30.04.2009.

PIANOS

A CENTURY *of* THURROCK

An engraving by Christopher Shiner of the Bull Inn in the old High Street, Grays, *c.* 1935. The inn was demolished in the 1960s. This was part of the 'sailor town'.

A CENTURY *of* THURROCK

BRIAN EVANS

SUTTON PUBLISHING

First published in 1999 by Sutton Publishing Limited

This new paperback edition first published in 2007 by
Sutton Publishing, an imprint of NPI Media Group
Cirencester Road · Chalford · Stroud · Gloucestershire · GL6 8PE

British Library Cataloguing in Publication Data
A catalogue record for this book is available from the British Library.

ISBN 978-0-7509-4940-8

Front endpaper: Waiting at the level crossing, Grays, *c*. 1912.
Back endpaper: Grays High Street today. The pedestrianisation of recent years takes the heat out of the traffic problem and puts people back in the centre of the town.
Half title page: The Fire Station at Orsett Road, Grays, opened in 1893, demolished in the 1970s.
Title page: A Grays wedding, 1920s. The couple have found a quiet spot behind the church. The photographer is S. Edwin Smith of 113 Clarence Road, Grays.

One of the Sun tugs – well known in Tilbury – which were pressed into service during the Second World War and took part in the Dunkirk evacuation.

Typeset in Photina.
Typesetting and origination by
Sutton Publishing.
Printed and bound in England.

Contents

LONDON TILBURY & SOUTHEND RAILWAY.

GENERAL ELECTION

1900.

To Superintendents, Station Masters, Inspectors, and all others in authority in all departments.

Every Servant of the Company having a Vote, and wishing to record it, is to be allowed sufficient time to do so, and arrangements must be made for this purpose.

No political meeting must be held, nor any electioneering bills or literature exhibited on the premises of the Company, and any canvassing or action (other than voting) in favor of any particular candidate, is strictly prohibited.

Copies of this notice to be exhibited in the Company's Workshops, Porters' Rooms, and elsewhere for the information of the staff.

ARTHUR L. STRIDE,

29th September, 1900. Managing Director.

There was a General Election in 1900 and the London, Tilbury and Southend Railway published an official staff notice about the arrangements for staff to vote.

Britain: A Century of Change

Children gathered around an early wireless set in the 1920s. The speed and forms of communication were to change dramatically as the century advanced. (*Barnaby's Picture Library*)

The delirious rejoicing at the news of the Relief of Mafeking, during the Boer War in May 1900, is a colourful historical moment. But, in retrospect, the introduction that year of the first motor bus was rather more important, signalling another major adjustment to town life. In the previous sixty years railway stations, post-and-telegraph offices, police and fire stations, gas works and gasometers, new livestock markets and covered markets, schools, churches, football grounds, hospitals and asylums, water pumping stations and sewerage plants had totally altered the urban scene, as the country's population tripled and over 70 per cent were born in or moved to the towns.

When Queen Victoria died in 1901, she was measured for her coffin by her grandson Kaiser Wilhelm, the London prostitutes put on black mourning and the blinds came down in the villas and terraces spreading out from the old town centres. These centres were reachable by train and tram, by the new bicycles and still newer motor cars, connected by the new telephone, and lit by gas or even electricity. The shops may have been full of British-made cotton and woollen clothing but the grocers and butchers were selling cheap Danish bacon, Argentinian beef, Australasian mutton, tinned or dried fish and fruit from Canada, California and South Africa. Most of these goods were carried in British-built-and-crewed ships, burning Welsh steam coal.

Women working as porters on the Great Western Railway, Paddington, *c.* 1917. *(W.L. Kenning/ Adrian Vaughan Collection)*

As the first decade moved on, the Open Spaces Act meant more parks, bowling greens and cricket pitches. The first state pensions came in, together with higher taxation and death duties. These were raised mostly to pay for the new Dreadnought battleships needed to maintain naval superiority over Germany, and deter them from war. But the deterrent did not work. The First World War transformed the place of women, as they took over many men's jobs. Its other legacies were the war memorials which joined the statues of Victorian worthies in main squares round the land. After 1918 death duties bit even harder and a quarter of England changed hands in a few years.

The multiple shop – the chain store – appeared in the high street: Sainsburys, Maypole, Lipton's, Home & Colonial, the Fifty Shilling Tailor, Burton, Boots, W.H. Smith. The shopper was spoilt for choice, attracted by the brash fascias and advertising hoardings for national brands like Bovril, Pears Soap, and Ovaltine. Many new buildings began to be seen, such as garages, motor showrooms, picture palaces (cinemas), 'palais de dance', and the bow-windowed, pebble-dashed, tile-hung, half-timbered houses that were built as ribbon-development along the roads and new bypasses or on the new estates nudging the green belts.

During the 1920s cars became more reliable and sophisticated as well as commonplace, with developments like the electric self-starter making them easier for women to drive. Who wanted to turn a crank handle in the new short skirt? This was, indeed, the electric age as much as the motor era. Trolley buses, electric trams and trains extended mass transport and electric light replaced gas in the street and the home, which itself was groomed by the vacuum cleaner.

Father and child cycling past Buckingham Palace on VE Day, 8 May 1945. (*Hulton Getty Picture Collection*)

A major jolt to the march onward and upward was administered by the Great Depression of the early 1930s. The older British industries – textiles, shipbuilding, iron, steel, coal – were already under pressure from foreign competition when this worldwide slump arrived, cutting exports by half in two years and producing 3 million unemployed (and still rising) by 1932. Luckily there were new diversions to alleviate the misery. The 'talkies' arrived in the cinemas; more and more radios and gramophones were to be found in people's homes; there were new women's magazines, with fashion, cookery tips and problem pages; football pools; the flying feats of women pilots like Amy Johnson; the Loch Ness Monster; cheap chocolate and the drama of Edward VIII's abdication.

Things were looking up again by 1936 and unemployment was down to 2 million. New light industry was booming in the Home Counties as factories struggled to keep up with the demand for radios, radiograms, cars and electronic goods including the first television sets. The threat from Hitler's Germany meant rearmament, particularly of the airforce, which stimulated aircraft and aero engine firms. If you were lucky and lived in the south, there was good money to be earned. A semi-detached house cost £450, a Morris Cowley £150. People may have smoked like chimneys but life expectancy, since 1918, was up by 15 years while the birth rate had almost halved. The fifty-four hour week was down to forty-eight hours and there were 9 million radio licences by 1939.

In some ways it is the little memories that seem to linger longest from the Second World War: the kerbs painted white to show up in the blackout, the rattle of ack-ack shrapnel on roof tiles, sparrows killed by

A family gathered around their television set in the 1950s. (*Hulton Getty Picture Collection*)

bomb blast, painting your legs brown and then adding a black seam down the back to simulate stockings. The biggest damage, apart from London, was in the south-west (Plymouth, Bristol) and the Midlands (Coventry, Birmingham). Postwar reconstruction was rooted in the Beveridge Report which set out the expectations for the Welfare State. This, together with the nationalisation of the Bank of England, coal, gas, electricity and the railways, formed the programme of the Labour government in 1945. At this time the USA was calling in its debts and Britain was beggared by the war, yet still administering its Empire.

Times were hard in the late 1940s, with rationing even more stringent than during the war. Yet this was, as has been said, 'an innocent and well-behaved era'. The first let-up came in 1951 with the Festival of Britain and then there was another fillip in 1953 from the Coronation, which incidentally gave a huge boost to the spread of TV. By 1954 leisure motoring had been resumed but the Comet – Britain's best hope for taking on the American aviation industry – suffered a series of mysterious crashes. The Suez debacle of 1956 was followed by an acceleration in the withdrawal from Empire, which had begun in 1947 with the Independence of India. Consumerism was truly born with the advent of commercial TV and most homes soon boasted washing machines, fridges, electric irons and fires.

The *Lady Chatterley* obscenity trial in 1960 was something of a straw in the wind for what was to follow in that decade. A collective loss of inhibition seemed to sweep the land, as stately home owners opened up, the Beatles and the Rolling Stones transformed popular music, and retailing, cinema and the theatre were revolutionised. Designers, hairdressers, photographers and models moved into places vacated by an Establishment put to flight by the new breed of satirists spawned by *Beyond the Fringe* and *Private Eye*.

In the 1970s Britain seems to have suffered a prolonged hangover after the excesses of the previous decade. Ulster, inflation and union troubles were not made up for by entry into the EEC, North Sea Oil, Women's Lib or, indeed, Punk Rock. Mrs Thatcher applied the corrective in the 1980s, as the country moved more and more from its old manufacturing base over to providing services, consulting, advertising, and expertise in the 'invisible' market of high finance or in IT. Britain entertained the world with *Cats*, *Phantom of the Opera*, *Four Weddings and a Funeral*, *The Full Monty*, *Mr Bean* and the *Teletubbies*.

Carnaby Street in the 1960s. (*Barnaby's Picture Library*)

The post-1945 townscape has seen changes to match those in the worlds of work, entertainment and politics. In 1956 the Clean Air Act served notice on smogs and pea-souper fogs, smuts and blackened buildings, forcing people to stop burning coal and go over to smokeless sources of heat and energy. In the same decade some of the best urban building took place in the 'new towns' like Basildon, Crawley, Stevenage and Harlow. Elsewhere open warfare was declared on slums and what was labelled inadequate, cramped, back-to-back, two-up, two-down, housing. The new 'machine for living in' was a flat in a high-rise block. The architects and planners who promoted these were in league with the traffic engineers, determined to keep the motor car moving whatever the price in multi-storey car parks, meters, traffic wardens and ring roads.

The Millennium Dome at Greenwich, 1999. (*Michael Durnan/Barnaby's Picture Library*)

The old pollutant, coal smoke, was replaced by petrol and diesel exhaust, and traffic noise. Even in the back garden it was hard to find peace as motor mowers, then leaf blowers and strimmers made themselves heard, and the neighbours let you share their choice of music from their powerful new amplifiers, whether you wanted to or not. Fast food was no longer only a pork pie in a pub or fish-and-chips. There were Indian curry houses, Chinese take-aways and American-style hamburgers, while the drinker could get away from beer in a wine bar. Under the impact of television the big Gaumonts and Odeons closed or were rebuilt as multi-screen cinemas, while the palais de dance gave way to discos and clubs.

From the late 1960s the introduction of listed buildings and conservation areas, together with the growth of preservation societies, put a brake on 'comprehensive redevelopment'. Now the new risk at the end of the 1990s is that town centres may die, as shoppers are attracted to the edge-of-town supermarkets surrounded by parking space, where much more than food and groceries can be bought. The ease of the one-stop shop represents the latest challenge to the good health of our towns. But with care, ingenuity and a determination to keep control of our environment, this challenge can be met.

Thurrock: An Introduction

During the last hundred years, the area now known collectively as Thurrock, consisting of what was once only one small town with a port and wharves surrounded by hundreds of acres of countryside dotted with villages, hamlets and lonely waterside haunts has several times astounded the world outside with its ability to conjure events so that formerly remote areas within its borders have rocketed from obscurity to nationwide and even worldwide fame.

The twentieth century could be said to have started early in Thurrock, as far back as 17 April 1886 when a far-sighted scheme to construct downstream docks at Tilbury, once an insignificant area of marshland in the Parish of Chadwell St Mary, was opened officially. By the recognised start of the new century these pioneering shipping facilities were set on a course of expansion which was to make them truly one of the wonders of this hectic century.

In 1908 the Port of London Authority took over from the old dock companies which had been in poor financial shape for some years. A Royal Commission, one of the last of Queen Victoria's reign and the first of the century, authorised by Royal Warrant of 21 June 1900, produced a report in June 1902. But various difficulties and opposition held up the transfer of powers until 1908. The new authority at once planned an extension to Tilbury Docks and a cargo jetty in the river. Tilbury was truly the first of Thurrock's wonders of the century. Its strategic importance having been recognised, this huge area of man-made sheltered water was to serve the world community. The value of such a facility to the nation in time of peace and war during the century cannot be overestimated. In the 1930s and after the Second World War many English emigrants started their journey to Australia from Tilbury. Later, immigrants from the West Indies came to Britain to fill gaps in the service industries beginning with the docking of the *Empire Windrush* at Tilbury. In the two wars thousands of troops left here for the war and many more returned through the quays.

Thurrock's Edwardian shopping expansion mainly took place in Grays where shopfronts were built on to what had once been houses. Today just one of these can be glimpsed at an upper storey level. It was certainly a time of consumer boom even though many families lived from hand to mouth, pay day never coming too soon as the money often ran out days early. However Thurrock's second wonder, the growing number of industries mainly along the Thames, was providing more employment opportunities and making the average home more prosperous. The Thames Paper Company (later Thames Board Mills), the Anglo-American Oil Company (later Esso), Tunnel Portland Cement and Kynoch's explosives are examples of factories that already existed at the beginning of the century. The First World War created further boom times because of increases in war production leading to many workers coming into the area. It also brought a new factory. During the war the British government invited two Dutch companies, the Jurgens and the Van den Berghs, to start up operations in Britain to overcome the threat of a fats shortage. So Jurgens opened a factory in Purfleet in 1918, and in 1927 merged with Van den Berghs. In this way European links already established in local industry were strengthened – a forerunner of today's Europeanisation of the economy.

A third wonder of Thurrock's century came with peace and restabilisation. In the 1920s new arterial roads were promoted – in Thurrock this particularly meant improvements and new routes for the London–Southend highway. At first these gleaming concrete two-way roads, often with a special cycle path alongside, were little used

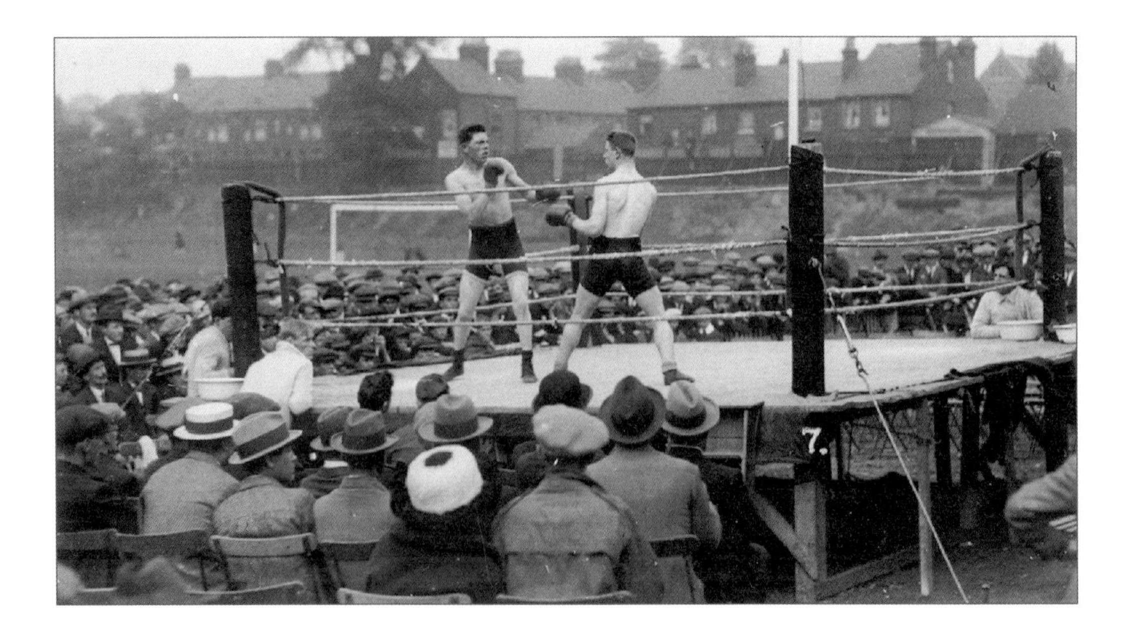

An attentive crowd watches Bill Eades of Grays and Johnny Gibbons of Bermondsey take part in a challenge boxing match at Grays Recreation Ground, Bridge Road. This early twentieth century bout followed on a long local sorting tradition. Many eighteenth and nineteenth century bare-knuckle contests were arranged on the marshes at Thames Haven and other spots to avoid the authorities, as such sport was then illegal. The photographer is the well-known local man, W.R. Menlove.

because of the relatively small numbers of cars on the road. A less expensive vehicle, the motor-cycle with sidecar, became very popular for small families and more buses, coaches and lorries began to fill these wonderful through routes – a portent of the heavy traffic at the end of the century. In spite of the arterial road and its route eastwards through Stifford to Lodge Lane and Blackshots, Grays Town was still rather cut off up to the 1960s, being bypassed by this highway through its northern suburbs. The approaches to Tilbury across the former marshland were also rather restricted. The original development was built around access to the docks mainly by rail – the railway was heavily involved, as a way of building its traffic in goods directly from the shipping at Tilbury. A new docks approach road took a long time to be built after the Second World War. Opening of the northern carriageway to link up with Woodview took place in August 1970.

Before the new Tilbury links came into being two more wonders of Thurrock and effective engines of change had appeared. The Aveley housing estate or Belhus estate signified a new order in the countryside to the north of Grays. This public housing scheme, one of several in the country outside London after the Second World War, was an amazing feat of large-scale planning. Nothing of its kind had been seen since the development of Dagenham in the 1920s. References to the Belhus estate before the late 1940s meant the parkland and farms of the venerable old mansion, the home of the Barrett-Lennard aristocratic family with its origins far back in history. Now in a short space of time the new housing, shops, public houses, social halls, churches suddenly took over the park and purlieus of the deserted mansion, which was finally demolished in 1957, while the housing and population around were still growing. In 1961 there were 22,212 inhabitants, many decanted from London, and this social experiment altered local perceptions forever, and tilted the population-mix towards young people. Not far away to the south as the 1960s began another long-delayed project, the tunnel under the Thames between Purfleet and Dartford, was steadily progressing. When it was inaugurated later in the '60s, it was as if a new door to and from Thurrock had been opened. Thurrock was now more accessible from everywhere in Britain and even the continent was brought nearer. The tunnel was impressive and put Thurrock on the map, just as some of the old quarry and extractive industries and even the cement works were in decline. Of many novel ideas connected with the tunnel one did not last: the provision of a special bus which carried cyclists and their bikes to and from the Kent side. At the time it seemed an excellent extra but was presumably overwhelmed by the number of cars and lorries using the tunnel in spite of the toll charge. Another translation to the modern age as the 1960s advanced was the conversion of the Grays branch railway from Pitsea to Barking and ultimately to London from steam to electric operation. The branch line which at that time ran as a through service all the way from Romford via Upminster was already using modern diesel units for the journey that usually ended at the bay platform in Grays. The diesel trains were a hint of modernity that had up till then eluded the main Stanford, Tilbury, Grays and Purfleet loop line.

In the 1960s also came the spectacular opening up of excavations at Mucking and in archaeological terms at least the spotlight of the world was turned on another wonder of Thurrock. Archaeologist M.U. Jones began a series of investigations of a major Saxon site spanning in the first instance thirteen years but in effect so much new information about the Saxon era and the ages of metals that preceded it came to light that the post-excavation ripples spread further and further. Archaeologists of every specialisation have been attracted to the evidence, and enquiries and follow-up research have been done in Britain, Germany and around the world. Thurrock Museum in Grays hosted much of the early post-excavation work and its displays, staff

The aptly named New Century Cycle Company shop at 56 High Street. The young lady may be the daughter of the manageress, Mrs Emily A. Carter. At the beginning of the century every household had one or more bicycles in the hallway or garden shed. They were the universal mode of transport for work, shopping and leisure.

The opening of Corringham Library, Lampits Hill in 1960. Thurrock Council had a rolling five-year plan for developing libraries at that time. Later this building was replaced by one in the new Corringham centre.

and research into the history of Thurrock through the ages is really yet another twentieth century wonder of Thurrock.

Since the 1970s wonder has followed wonder locally, as the gradual regeneration of Grays with its pedestrianisation, shopping mall and public sculpture, housing renewal and building of the new Council Complex north of the railway together with the new road bridge over the railway have taken shape. Even more startling has been the transformation at the beginning of the 1990s of the old chalk pit and industrial area into the gigantic Lakeside shopping complex with its 1.3 million square feet of trading space. A magnificent feat of engineering – the Queen Elizabeth II Bridge now complements the tunnels at what is now termed the Dartford Crossing.

Just to prove that Thurrock has not finished with the business of wonders a new housing area of phenomenal size known as Chafford Hundred is now, as the century ends, growing between Grays and Lakeside, and a brand new railway station on the Upminster branch has been built and opened to serve both the houses and the Lakeside shopping centre

A feature of Thurrock Thameside at the beginning of the century was the Boys' Training Ships. *Above*: boys on the *Exmouth* cleaning the decks. *Below*: *Exmouth* lads learning the morse code.

The New Century

The Grays Co-operative Society central premises when it was one of the most impressive buildings in the town, *c.* 1904. The Society was begun in 1884 by workers at Grays Chalk Quarries. In 1901 the membership had reached 3,000 and members were joining at the rate of about 100 a year. The attraction of the movement was not just the dividend that was regularly returned to members – quite a high proportion of the profits were put into an educational fund and a reading room and a meeting room were other benefits.

The No. 2 Branch of the Co-op at West Thurrock with its aproned staff.

The Assembly Room at the central shop and premises.

Tilbury Ferry at its mooring, *c.* 1903. There had been a ferry between here and the Kent side of the river for centuries. But in the twentieth century just beginning communications of every kind were to be key in opening up Thurrock's economy and putting the area on the commercial map. The publisher is the appropriately named E.J. Shipman of Tilbury.

The large ships here give the scale for measuring the immense area of water even in this one western branch of Tilbury Docks. A storage van on the dockside bears the legend W. Moll, Rotterdam.

Beside the docks is this quiet area around the World's End public house and Tilbury Fort. This photograph from the beginning of the century shows an unfamiliar beach scene without the high sea wall that cuts off the river view today.

Heinke's diving gear pump is proving its worth at Tilbury Docks in July 1905. A picture that lifts a corner on the hidden world of developing technology as the twentieth century gathers pace.

Looking up the High Street, past the many wooden vernacular buildings from various periods of history, *c.* 1902. This area was near the Thames so it was one that mariners knew well. In the public houses and inns that once abounded you would also find many bargemen – Grays had one of the largest fleets of sailing barges based nearby.

Another prospect of the old High Street showing the western side, early in the century.

The old chalk quarries at Meeson's Lane, *c.* 1904. There was still a living for chalk workers: Grays had so much chalk it was almost an honorary but detached part of Kent.

The Queen's Hotel *c.* 1908 when it stood proudly at the bottom of the newer part of High Street at the junction with Orsett Road. It was Seabrook Brewery's pride and joy (and the superior licensed house up to the 1960s at least). It had cost £7,000 to build in the days when that was a big sum. It was rebuilt after a serious fire in 1890 and was a real landmark in Grays for more than half of the twentieth century.

A rooftop view of the northern part of Grays High Street, over the railway, *c.* 1908.

A view of the railway station at Grays, *c.* 1908.

Thameshaven in the early 1900s was a remote station on the marshes at the south-eastern end of Thurrock. I has been used for railway operation, transporting products from the industry here, throughout the twentieth century. There is a link with the main Stanford-le-Hope to Grays line.

Corringham, on the Corringham Light Railway, was another area remote from the mainstream of traffic in the 1920s. Its role was to carry workers the relatively short distance across the marshes to Kynochtown (named after Kynoch's explosives manufacturers), later changed to Coryton (after the petroleum importing firm of Cory's). The line was linked with the Thameshaven branch.

The grass begins to grow over the tracks at Coryton station. There were gaps in operation as the works changed from Kynoch's to Cory's and then the Vacuum Oil Co., later known as Mobil Oil. The line closed to passengers in the 1950s.

Grays High Street is full of incident here, *c.* 1914. Although there is a motor-cycle with a sidecar parked on the left, the dearth of other traffic allows the pedestrians to wander freely in the road – in 1999 pedestrianisation has made this easy again. The Empire Theatre is the white building on the right.

Grays beach has a real holiday atmosphere, *c.* 1910. Although an artificial creation it has been enjoyed by successive generations of children along with the refreshment rooms, paddling pool and promenade with seats nearby as a real holiday place near to home.

High Street, Aveley from Ship Lane Corner in 1910. The photographer is being watched with interest – he is producing a postcard for Finbow's shop (on left) to sell.

The whole Thurrock area at the start of the century had a strong tradition of bandsmanship equivalent to that in many industrial areas of the north. Here, in about 1910, the Tilbury Band proudly line up in their distinctive uniforms, with their instruments ready, one of a legion of such bands eager to prove its worth in performance.

The training ship *Exmouth* boys sit in their boat which is carried on wheels and drawn by horse and cart in the Grays Carnival Procession pre-1914. This scene is at the corner of Brooke Road and Orsett Road.

In the Thames off Grays *c*. 1912 the picture is filled by three types of object. Apart from the river and the sky there are the bulk of the training ship *Exmouth*, a great host of small boats and sailing barges and the chimneys of works on the Kent shore.

Not so often seen is a photograph of the second training ship, *Exmouth II*, shown here *c*. 1916.

Two years before the start of the First World War a wave of industrial unrest in the country provoked the Dock Strike of 1912. Here is part of an important procession in Grays High Street in support of the dockers. The Temperance Silver Band is in the van of the march which was as good as any Lord Mayor's Show. The man with the collection box is masked to prevent victimisation by the employers. He was right to be cautious as the ever-on-the-lookout photographer, W.R. Menlove, has gained access to the window or balcony above the shop and captured the moment for ever. The London and Provincial Bank in the background became Barclays, which was demolished in the last few decades of the century to make way for the new one-way road link section between the railway and the northern part of the High Street.

This is the spectacle of unfurling the flag at Purfleet to celebrate the coronation of George V, 22 June 1911. Hats off and three cheers! In the days before radio and television local people set great store by such events and it was a way of marking a very special occasion to arrange parades with any service personnel available in the vicinity together with speeches by local notables. Instead of the jeans and tee-shirts that are worn by many today we have a surprisingly formal dressed-up approach to match the uniforms. Purfleet was a real community where everyone knew each other but society was also stratified into levels of class where everybody knew his place. In the war to come some of the bonds holding together this kind of society were to be loosened.

A fine day at the bathing pond, Grays beach, 1908. How many of the boys would be young soldiers fighting in France less than a decade on? How many would survive?

Town and Country

Rectory Road, Little Thurrock, 1913. With its comparatively new houses this street looks quite suburban. There were many Victorian and earlier roads in the vicinity that were much quainter, with back alleys and strange windings that suggested a landscape of 100 years before. Some of this atmosphere lasted till quite recent times, with unmade roads and individual architecture.

Floods at the River Mardyke at Stifford, 10 March 1914.

The Corner Shop, East Street, South Stifford, *c.* 1909. The display window is quite an impressive one for such local premises.

Five past eleven a.m. by the shopping parade opposite St Margaret's at Stanford-le-Hope, probably *c.* 1914. The writer of the postcard a few years later in 1916 says he has 'not seen any Zepp[elin]s yet'.

A pig in clover at Stanford-le-Hope, 1908.

Riverview Cottages next to the Post Office, Purleet. Other shops ensured that most errands were very local in 1914.

Almost a rural scene by the Fox and Goose, West Thurrock, *c.* 1914. It is only prevented from being one by the various terraces including St George's Terrace, London Road, part of the ribbon development along this old line of communication with the outside world. Again the two local shops provide the simpler necessities of households of the time with their less sophisticated diet, no doubt supplemented by rabbits and game from local fields and disused chalk pits.

Two views of rural Horndon, *c.* 1908. The village, set on its hilltop ridge, was something of a law to itself, in the early years of the century. The top photograph looks down the hill past the Bell Inn, while the bottom view looks up towards the main part of the village. The mix and grouping of buildings from many eras is something that has to grow over centuries and cannot be created overnight. Looking back it delights the eye in the same way as scenes from nature often do.

High View Avenue, Grays – definitely one of the better class streets in which to live, 1904.

The Cottage in Dell Road, Grays. This was another old chalk pit. Dell House at the end had been the home of Alfred Russell Wallace, a naturalist whose ideas were used in Darwin's famous work about evolution. This view dates from about 1904.

Orsett as it was, 1919. The village has not changed as much as many other places in Thurrock. Modern Orsett is featured later in this book.

A. Smith's shop is on the right of this 1916 view of Orsett.

Signpost corner at South Ockendon has an impressive motor car as a talking point, 1918. Very often at this time the only car belonged to the local general practitioner.

Industrial Purfleet, laid out along the river bank, showed only one side of the character of this very individual area with others being its housing, Botany Gardens leisure area and Royal Garrison.

Tilbury Seamen's Hospital, *c.* 1916. The hospital was part of another of Thurrock's colourful and diverse places. Tilbury had grown to a town from obscurity. The presence of shipping meant that there were a number of institutions working on behalf of seafarers. The hospital was largely supported by charity collections and money was raised by the Dreadnought Seamen's Hospital Society at Greenwich.

Part of Dock Road, Tilbury, *c.* 1912, with the Roman Catholic Church and Presbytery. Trees have been planted to soften the rather bare aspect of the early town. Many of the original workers who constructed the docks and railway system were Irish Catholics who stayed and made their contribution to its culture. Some of the local names reflect these founding fathers, among them 'Feenan Highway' and 'Brennan Road'.

Excited children on a day out to Cox's Tea Gardens at Purfleet, *c.* 1908. The party may be from an orphanage or home for disabled children, usually known at this period as a Crippleage. Coming to Purfleet, seeing the ships on the river, visiting the gardens in the old chalk pits and perhaps being taken to the top of Botany Hill together with the tea was a favourite excursion and treat for parties of all kinds. At one stage the resort was known as Cox and Palmer's Tea Garden and the proprietors publicised their premises by issuing photographic postcards.

In 1919, the quiet village of Fobbing was not as accessible as Purfleet, being some way from a railway station. Later on the arterial road of the 1920s and the hiking craze of the 1930s unveiled its charms to a select few.

Called to Service

Top: A Gotha bomber. In 1917 raids on Thurrock were being carried out by aeroplanes which had replaced the airships. Zeppelins attacked on only six nights but forty people died and about seventy were injured. On Wednesday 13 June a large-scale attack on London was mounted from Germany by twenty-two Gotha bombers. Three bombers diverted defending aircraft by attacking Margate and Shoeburyness and letting themselves be chased back over the Channel. The others flew in over Foulness via Brentwood, using the Thames to guide them to London. They bombed a Poplar school, killing eighteen children and seriously wounding thirty. Two trains were destroyed at Liverpool Street station. This led to parents in Grays to believe that the Germans could target all schools. Anxious mothers tried to rush into Bridge Road School after an aircraft warning sounded the next day at 2.40 p.m.
Bottom: A British BE 2c fighter plane. It took these older planes 55 minutes to reach a height of 10,000 ft. The German bombers had a crew of three and a 72 ft wingspan, flying at a great height and reaching almost the same speed as the British fighters. It was a great problem for the Royal Flying Corps and Royal Naval Air Service pilots to know how to cope with the situation. Even the newest Sopwith Camel aircraft with a top speed of 113 mph needed twelve minutes to get to the required altitude.

Before the war, in the first decade of the century, the people of Grays went about their business little dreaming of the troubled times ahead. During the war the station area and High Street were often full of soldiers coming and going to and from the battle front in France, and also various other military establishments and camps in the area. Scenes of great joy for 'Tommies' coming home on leave would be witnessed and corresponding ones of sadness when they left to rejoin the conflict. Between 800 and 1,000 locals paid the supreme price of the war. Other families welcomed back fathers, sons, brothers and cousins who were disabled either mentally or physically.

Entrance to the Garrison, Purfleet. Originally a small number of soldiers had guarded the powder magazines which had been located here for over 100 years. It was one of the first areas to see a build-up of troops in 1914 – a huge tented camp appeared overnight, housing hundreds of soldiers. Although the initial contingent soon left for France as part of the British Expeditionary Force they were replaced by others and the quaint old village of Purfleet became used to the continual presence of a large force of recruits.

Some local men joined the Grays Company of the 2nd Battalion, Chelmsford Regiment, seen here on Whit Monday, 1915.

Postal staff at Belhus Park Camp, 1915. The army authorities established post offices in many camps because of the substantial amount of mail being received and sent. This helped to lessen the isolation of men posted away from home and boosted morale.

A postcard sent in January 1916 of Purfleet Schools by a recruit named Horace to his aunt in Bryfield, Northamptonshire. The address is No. 2182 'B' Company, Hut 36, A Lines, Purfleet. The message reads 'Just a card to let you know I am well. I hope you are. I was home this week end. Much love. Your Affectionate Nephew.'

The ferry and shipping at Tilbury, *c.* 1912. The postcard was sent on 20 February 1915 by 'Harry' to his sister while aboard the Royal Mail ship *Walmer Castle* at Tilbury. The message reads: 'I am writing to tell you that we are almost ready for sailing now'. Although the German submarine threat was not so universal as later in the war, there was obviously some risk as the vessel made its way out to sea.

Crowds wait near the Grays Unionist Club to watch volunteers for Kitchener's Army march to the railway station in March 1916, led by the boys' band from the training ship *Exmouth*.

A postcard of the monastery, Stanford-Le-Hope, which was posted by a daughter to her wounded father 19885 Private A.A. Whitehead, City Hospital, Lodge Moor, Sheffield – the picture may have reminded him of the country for which he was fighting. Posted on 16 August 1917 from Stanford the little girl writes in large script: 'Dear Daddy, I am glad you are getting better. I am having a nice time myself. Love From Winnie. XXXXXXXXX'

The Thames Paper Works, seen before the First World War. Later to become the Thames Board Mills this was, like other factories in Thurrock and elsewhere, turned over to wartime operation to produce anything that would assist the war effort. With imports restricted it no doubt produced paper for government memos and official notices as well as more warlike products.

Women workers at Thames Paper Mills. So many younger men were being recruited for the forces that women began to fill the gaps in large numbers and were tackling manual jobs once thought unsuitable for their sex. In the picture are essential male supervisors and older and medically unfit men not required for armed service. By 1916 women had become an essential part of the labour force.

An information sheet issued during the war carried this photograph pointing out the key roles being played by women in the wartime factories.

The SS Clan *Mackintosh* lying off Purfleet Timber Wharf. On 3 February 1915 another Clan vessel which had been converted into an armed merchant cruiser – the HMS Clan *McNaughton* – went down in a storm in the North Atlantic. Thirty-five local men were among the crew drowned. George Street, Grays now had nine new widows. Another vessel, the SS Clan *Campbell*, was torpedoed by a German submarine in April 1916. She had been a regular visitor to Tilbury. Fortunately on this occasion all the ship's crew were safely plucked from the waters of the Mediterranean Sea.

British submarine 'L' Class No. 27, built as part of the Emergency Programme, 1916. The British Navy was struggling to match the German submarine fleet. The L27 had an armament of one 4-inch gun and four bow torpedo tubes. She was built by Vickers and completed at Sheerness, further along the river on the Kent shore. Some of the British designs were quirky – it was hard enough to be a submariner without poor design hampering the working of such vessels. An earlier vessel L2 was broken up at Ward's Yard, Grays, in 1930 (see *Around Grays in Old Photographs*, p. 50).

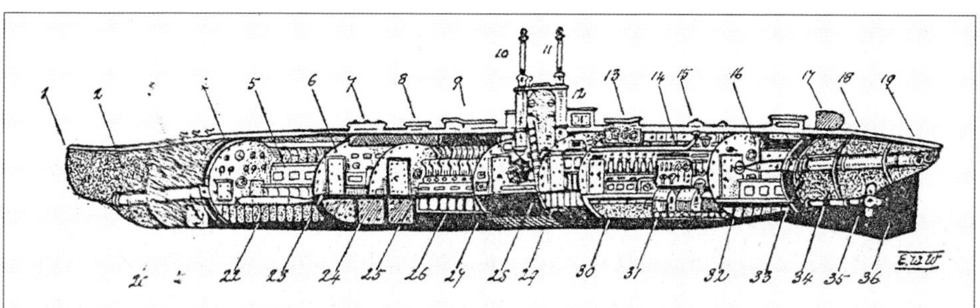

SECTIONAL VIEW OF THE INTERIOR OF A GERMAN SUBMARINE.

1. Bow. 2. Tank. 3. Surface anchor. 4. Torpedo compensating tank. 5. Bow torpedo compartment. 6. Officers' quarters. 7. Torpedo hatch. 8. Escape hatch. 9. Quick-firing gun, folded down. 10 and 11. Periscopes. 12. Conning-tower. 13. Quick-firer, folded down. 14. Exhaust pipe. 15. Sealed exhaust. 16. Stern torpedo compartment. 17. Rudder. 18. Torpedo tubes. 19. Stern. 20. Bow torpedo tubes. 21. Submerged anchor. 22. Spare torpedo. 23. Living quarters. 24. Oil fuel tanks. 25. Quarters for crew. 26. Accumulators. 27. Water ballast. 28. Working chamber. 29. Accumulators. 30. Lubricating oil tanks. 31. Electric motors. 32. Tanks. 33 and 34. Water ballast tanks. 35. Propeller. 36. Steering rudder.

German submarines or U-boats had already been responsible for taking the lives of seamen from the Thurrock area when on 1 February 1917 the German government embarked on a policy of unrestricted submarine warfare, resulting in a frightening increase in marine casualties.

This map shows the area of the North Sea and Atlantic blockade imposed by the German naval high command.

Zeppelin airship in flight. The year 1916 was particularly noted for Zeppelin raids. On Friday 31 March there was an airship raid on Lincolnshire, Essex and Suffolk. Seventeen civilian and thirty-one military deaths were recorded. Anti-aircraft batteries at Purfleet opened fire just before 10 p.m. on L 15, spotted in the night sky. The airship, hit by the guns, turned heavily, trying to make its escape back along the Thames, dropping bombs in fields at Thurrock. Kynochtown's two 6-pounders had also fired at the Zeppelin, along with guns at Thameshaven, Erith, Plumstead and Dartford. Royal Flying Corps planes were also in flight searching out the target.

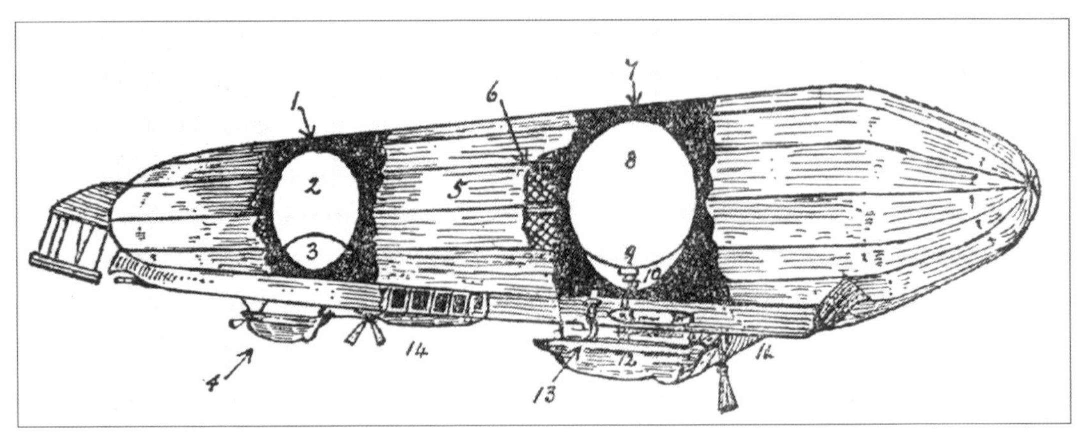

Zeppelin cross-section. The L 15 went out of control and crashed in the sea. After an hour or so, apart from one who drowned, the crew of nineteen was saved by trawlers operating in the area. The amazing total of 353 service personnel involved in this effort of 'downing' the airship each received a gold medallion marking their success.

Heinrich Mathy, a redoubtable German airship warrior, was in charge of L 31 which attacked London on 24 September 1916 with ten other Zeppelins. He evaded the guns and other defences and dropped bombs on Mitcham, Streatham, Brixton and Kennington before making his way back to Germany. Two other airships in this raid came to grief. One of them, L 32, was intercepted over south Essex. Lt Sowrey from Sutton's Farm airfield, Hornchurch, attacked and set light to the airship's buoyancy tanks which were filled with hydrogen. After dropping her bombs, which fell partly on Aveley and South Ockendon, the vessel caught light from end to end and fell at Great Burstead near Billericay, killing all twenty-two crew.

Bathe De Brandon of the Royal Flying Corps who attacked L 15, climbing 9,000 ft above the airship and dropping explosive darts on her, 31 March 1916.

A graphic design from Perfect's *Hornchurch during the Great War*, which shows a Zeppelin night raid and the anti-aircraft defences (searchlights and mounted guns).

This card of Aveley High Street was posted home by a soldier who ironically dated it 'Guy Fawkes Night 1917' – well aware of the Guy Fawkes displays seen on the battle front in France. He writes 'There has been nothing said re removal of the "Mobilisation Order", so I do not know if my (home leave) pass will be cancelled or postponed.'

Gordon Terrace, West Thurrock. About 150 German prisoners were encamped at Wouldham's Quarry at West Thurrock in 1918. It was quite a shock for the inhabitants when a number of these were taken to the Post Office wearing their uniforms each day, casually guarded by a 'Tommy' brandishing a fixed bayonet.

The training ship *Warspite* suffered a serious fire at Grays in 1918. This led the Governors to lease the Tilbury Hotel for three years to house the 200 young lads from the vessel. Did this lead to a less spartan lifestyle and a relaxation of some of the discipline aboard?

The Tilbury Hotel was owned and run by the Port of London authority after the creation of this body in 1908. It was known around the world by international passengers who in peacetime travelled by the great liners, the precursors of the frequent air travellers of today. The boys would still have had an unequalled view of the river traffic in shipping. Its solitary position at the head of the docks might have made it a target for German bombers, but it survived the First World War only to be destroyed over 20 years later in the Second.

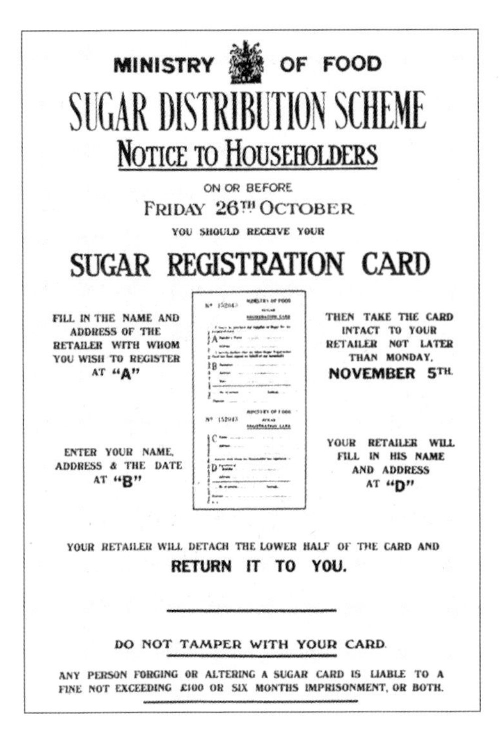

MINISTRY OF FOOD

SUGAR DISTRIBUTION SCHEME

NOTICE TO HOUSEHOLDERS

ON OR BEFORE
FRIDAY 26TH OCTOBER
YOU SHOULD RECEIVE YOUR

SUGAR REGISTRATION CARD

FILL IN THE NAME AND ADDRESS OF THE RETAILER WITH WHOM YOU WISH TO REGISTER AT "A"

THEN TAKE THE CARD INTACT TO YOUR RETAILER NOT LATER THAN MONDAY, NOVEMBER 5TH.

ENTER YOUR NAME, ADDRESS & THE DATE AT "B"

YOUR RETAILER WILL FILL IN HIS NAME AND ADDRESS AT "D"

YOUR RETAILER WILL DETACH THE LOWER HALF OF THE CARD AND RETURN IT TO YOU.

DO NOT TAMPER WITH YOUR CARD

ANY PERSON FORGING OR ALTERING A SUGAR CARD IS LIABLE TO A FINE NOT EXCEEDING £100 OR SIX MONTHS IMPRISONMENT, OR BOTH.

Sugar rationing notice. Towards the end of 1917 the problems in obtaining sugar led to the introduction of sugar coupons which allowed ½ lb per head per week. In 1918 there was great joy when an extra 4 oz were allowed for Christmas week.

This humorous postcard shows an enormous queue waiting to purchase potatoes, and links this to a line from a popular song of the day. The first real scarcity of the war was that of potatoes in spring 1917. This was partially caused by the demand for seed potatoes for planting. Food shortages became worse and police were ordered to disperse lines of people waiting outside local shops before 7.30 in the morning. Although it was winter time, in some instances mothers sent their children to get an early place in the queue by 5 a.m.

The war brought a boom time to shops like this one at Kynochtown. The munitions factory built in 1898 on the marshes beyond Fobbing had expanded rapidly. It was employing hundreds of women on twelve-hour shifts – many were earning their own money for the first time. In addition 6,000 extra men had been recruited for vital war production.

Men employed at Kynoch's cordite production line on the 'B' shift, July 1917. In spite of the unhealthy atmosphere which meant that workers were sometimes overcome and had to recover in the open air before resuming, there was consternation in 1918 when the possibility of closure became known. A public meeting was held in the cinema at Stanford-le-Hope and it was pointed out that many families' survival depended on employment at the factory. The new cordite works had in fact only opened a couple of years previously.

The War Memorial on its prominent site in the centre of Grays honours the men who fell in the war. It is hard at this distance in time to realise the effect on families of such devastation to a whole generation of mostly young men. Not only were there many widows but the loss of fiancés and boyfriends meant that hundreds of young women never married because there was a surplus of females.

A gravestone in St Peter and Paul's churchyard records the death of Major E. Warren at Cambrai in one of the significant battles of the First World War on 29 March 1918. The fact that his father lived on to the age of eighty-one, fourteen years later, in spite of having fought in four dangerous campaigns, aptly points out the poignancy of the loss of younger men in France, a whole generation being wiped out in five years.

Stanford-le-Hope War Memorial shortly after its construction represents the unique way in which Britain remembers its dead through several thousand local village memorials, at which a service is held year after year. Such monuments contrasted strangely in their modernity with the local vernacular buildings from centuries before. Villagers would never again be so innocent or cut off from what was going on elsewhere. The mindset of a whole people changed. From now on news from all over the world would be followed more closely through the medium of the press, the new radio broadcasting (then known as 'wireless') and newsreel film. The local population became more cynical and restless, avid for novelty and tired of simple old-fashioned ways.

New Hopes, New Prosperity

H. Clements stands in the doorway of his shop. He is listed in Kelly's 1922 directory at 8–10 The Broadway, Grays. In the 1920s traders gradually re-established themselves after the artificial boom of wartime. There was still a demand for shoe repairers but multiple chains established stores in the town selling mass-produced shoes which led to a decline in local shoemaking. Demand continued, however, for special shoes from the many people whose feet were disabled by the more common birth defects of the time and, of course, from the thousands who had received leg and foot injuries in the war.

A railway carriage hoisted between shore and ship at Tilbury in the 1920s. After a slow start Britain's exports gradually revived after the war.

Transferring passengers by tender to the *Esperance Bay* at Tilbury in 1928. Many great liners of the sea were using Tilbury as a port of call.

Grays Athletic Football Club was a smart and successful outfit – the team, officials and supporters line up for the 1921/2 Season.

The jetty and tanks at Shell Haven. The postcard was sent by a father to his son in October 1922. He writes 'this is where crude oil is stored when it comes by ship to England to be made into petrol'.

The old-style quiet and winding Southend Road at Stanford-le-Hope, *c.* 1920.

The new concrete highway, still gleaming white and not heavily used, also has a few bends as it rolls towards Southend at Corringham in the late 1920s.

The Southend Road at Grays with a solitary car in view, 1929. Traffic was slowly growing encouraged by the new mass-produced models, aimed at the middle and better-off working classes. More and more arterial roads were being built to shorten routes between towns.

A quiet time at South Ockendon station, August 1921. The railways had been run down by intense wartime traffic. The Government grouped the old railway companies into four rationalised groups which operated from 1924 and were able to make economies of scale.

Ruskin Road, Chadwell St Mary, *c.* 1929. Between the wars there was a large increase in housing, both public and private, in most areas of Thurrock.

This building seen here in 1999 was during the 1920s the busy main office of the Grays and Tilbury Gas Company (24–28 Orsett Road). The Gas Works can still be seen in London Road. At this period most people used gas for cooking and there were still Victorian and Edwardian houses with gas lighting even after the Second World War.

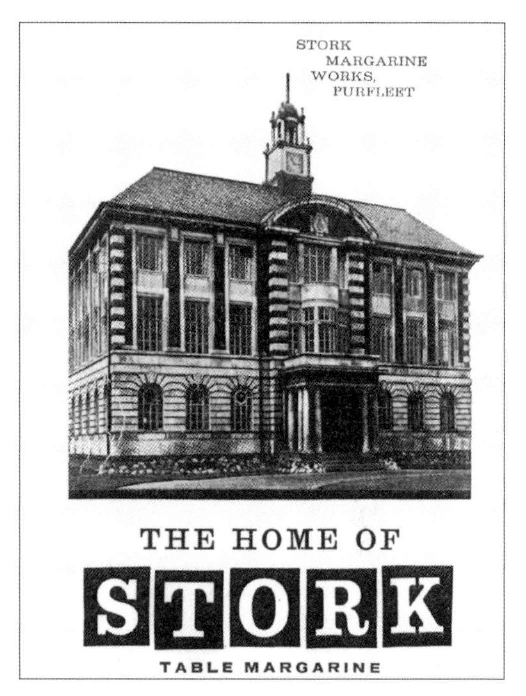

Van den Berghs and Jurgens, the very well known Thurrock business, built its office in a Dutch style near its factory at Purfleet and became a household name. Margarine was not readily accepted when first introduced, and took a long time to gain popularity.

Another Thurrock brand was Thors Oak, products of Seabrook's Brewery located south of the railway, east of the foot of Bridge Road. This was bought out in 1929 and closed down. The Grays Co-operative Society took over part of the buildings.

A new Post Office was built at the beginning of the 1930s in George Street, Grays. Few people who were able to save then had a bank or building society account, but many had a Post Office Savings account and the Post Office was a busy place. Seen in 1999 the revamped Post Office offers many new services. Before 1930 the main office was in New Road.

The building of the Ritz Cinema in the 1930s brought the number of cinemas in Grays to three.

A new style luxury limited-stop bus service to London. The Green Line coach was inaugurated in the 1930s by the new London Passenger Transport Board.

Still surviving at first floor level, in 1999, is the striking 1930s-style shopfront of Burtons the Tailors, though the firm no longer trades from these premises. The shop is typical of various national chain traders who set up in Grays between the wars. There was however still a high proportion of local traders compared with other towns.

A Thurrock council housing estate in the 1930s. Thurrock Urban District was formed on 1 April 1936, and took over powers from previous areas such as Tilbury and Purfleet which were previously local council areas.

An advertisement for a private developer's houses and bungalows in the late 1930s.

The Bata factory on the marshes. Bata came to East Tilbury in 1933, building not only a factory making rubber and leather footwear but creating a whole community. The community included a housing estate of several hundred semi-detached homes, shopping facilities, a hotel, a cinema, sports facilities, social hall, primary school, farm and dairy and a whole range of other amenities.

A 1930s Harris advertisement. Harris was a Grays family firm which was run from an office at 6 Parker Road in an ordinary house: it was already an ambitious advertiser in the 1930s. By the mid-70s it had become a transport complex handling 15,000 tons of freight and 400,000 passengers a year. In July/August 1976 the firm launched a travel agency which still trades today. They have expanded their bus operations in the 1990s into the London Transport region, running buses between various towns such as Ilford and Romford.

The Grays Temperance Silver Band with mascot and trophy, 1939.

The People's War and After

German bomber's view of the Thames.

Heavy guns were put in position in many locations in Thurrock during the Second World War. Thurrock's open spaces provided some good locations for anti-aircraft emplacements and most were in place by 1940. N 13 was at Bucklands, East Tilbury, and was furnished with two 3.7 inch guns. Many of the ancillary buildings still remain and are used for farm buildings. There were also travelling guns on lorries. Other sites were at Orsett, Aveley, North Ockendon, west of Hogg Lane (Old Belmont land), Thames Haven, Stanford-le-Hope and Shell Haven.

The Bata shoe factory with its busy community was in quite a vulnerable position, as German bombers flew down the Thames along the Thurrock banks of the Thames. The company formed its own Local Defence Volunteers, the predecessors of the Home Guard. They had to drill with dummy rifles made by the skilled last carpenter at Bata out of spare wood. They started without any uniforms.

Sun tugs well known in Tilbury were pressed into service for the war effort. The complete Sun tug fleet which worked throughout the Port of London pre-war went to rescue the British Army and others from Dunkirk. This remarkable emergency evacuation to rescue soldiers lined up on the beaches, under continual shell fire and dive bomber attack, was an important moment in the war, turning defeat into a kind of victory.

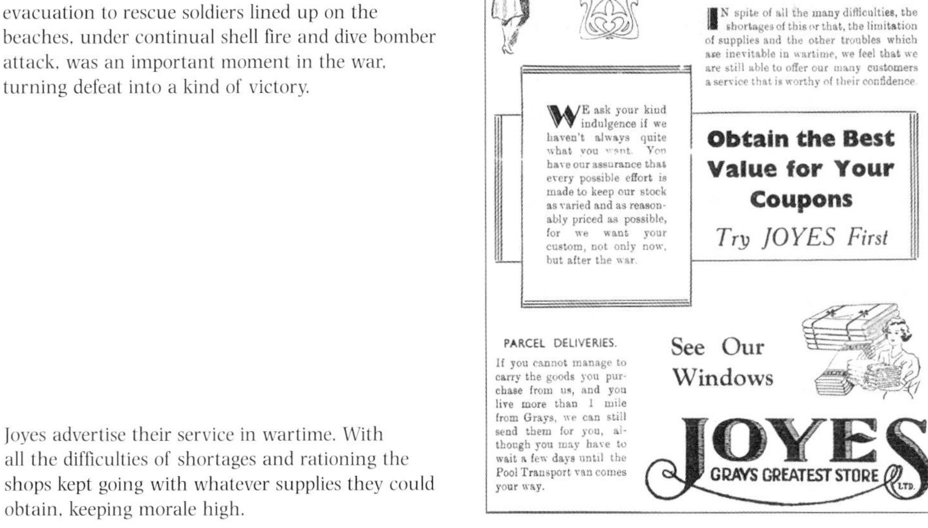

Joyes advertise their service in wartime. With all the difficulties of shortages and rationing the shops kept going with whatever supplies they could obtain, keeping morale high.

Bomb damage at the Co-operative premises.

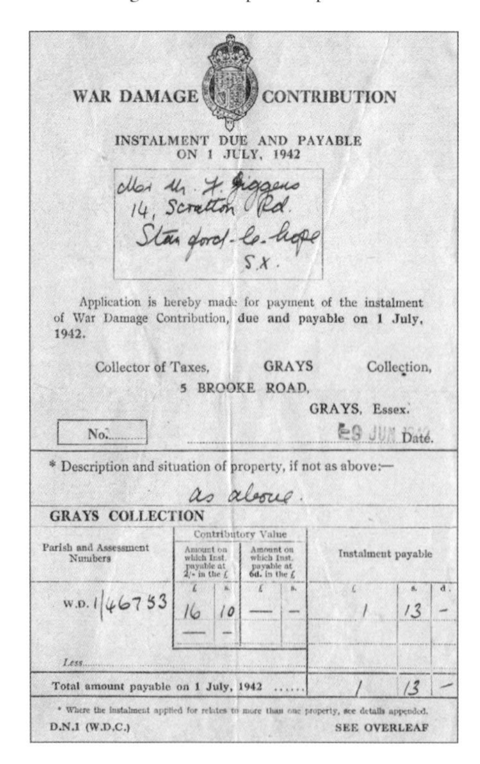

WAR DAMAGE CONTRIBUTION

INSTALMENT DUE AND PAYABLE
ON 1 JULY, 1942

Mrs M. F. Jiggens
14, Scratton Rd.
Stanford-le-hope
S.X.

Application is hereby made for payment of the instalment of War Damage Contribution, due and payable on 1 July, 1942.

Collector of Taxes, GRAYS Collection,
5 BROOKE ROAD,
GRAYS, Essex.

No.......... 29 JUN 1942 Date.

* Description and situation of property, if not as above:—

as above.

GRAYS COLLECTION

Parish and Assessment Numbers	Contributory Value: Amount on which Inst. payable at 2/- in the £ (£)	(s.)	Contributory Value: Amount on which Inst. payable at 6d. in the £ (£)	(s.)	Instalment payable (£)	(s.)	(d.)
W.D. 1/46753	16	10	—	—	1	13	–
	—	—					
Less							
Total amount payable on 1 July, 1942					1	13	–

* Where the instalment applied for relates to more than one property, see details appended.

D.N.1 (W.D.C.) SEE OVERLEAF

Certain individuals received a form during the war demanding war damage tax. A much smaller proportion of the working population paid income tax pre-war.

Quarry Hill today. On 26 February 1941 this was the scene of air raid incidents. A string of four bombs landed on Grays, one falling next to the side wall of the Ritz cinema which can be seen on the left. As usual when the warning siren in the town sounded a caption was displayed on a corner of the screen: 'Raid in Progress'. It was up to each person to decide whether to stay and watch the film or make for shelter. As the noise of the bomb reverberated through the walls, people threw themselves to the floor. Some soon left but others stayed, watching the film to the bitter end.

Films at the three local cinemas in February 1945 towards the end of the war when Hitler's V2 rocket weapons were descending on London and the south-east. At the beginning of the war places of entertainment were closed for a short time. When it was realised how important these were for public morale they were reopened. Not many people were killed while enjoying themselves – it was safer to be indoors when a raid was on, rather than being cut to pieces by flying shrapnel in the street.

Palmers Avenue, Grays, scene of an interesting report by a press informant in 1944 who witnessed the tremendous build-up of troops and armoured vehicles in the district just before D-Day. Nearly every plot of vacant land was taken over by military vehicles. 'Big encampments sprang up overnight and field kitchens and other necessary accommodation were built to cater for the troops. Many of the men never left their vehicles and slept in them at night-time. Two or three days before the announcement that a landing (in France) had been effected, military traffic increased considerably. . . . All through the nights the engines of war continued on their way. On one particular occasion just before midnight I heard a terrific noise in the distance. At the top of Palmers Avenue I waited and there, coming in the light of a clouded moon, along Southend Road, I saw a spectacle the like of which I had never seen before. Huge tanks weighing several tons, with their smokescreen attachments, were belching forth acrid smoke which rolled in clouds above the vehicles.'

The various chalk pits in the neighbourhood of Grays made ideal resting places for men and armour awaiting the order to embark for France. The general public were kept in the dark about what was going on for fear of spies giving the game away. 'Months before D-Day there was more than usual activity at the [Tilbury] Docks. Hundreds of men were drafted into the district on work of great importance, the nature of which was not yet fully disclosed. Rumours ran rife of course and there was considerable speculation. . . . So far as the general public were concerned, Tilbury was a closed book, and anything connected with the docks was referred to in whispers – a wink or a nod conveyed much in those days. There was a cheerful spirit of expectancy . . . and most people, even if they were in no way concerned with the work, felt a little proud of being associated with such an important district.'

Rationing of all kinds continued for the people of Thurrock, as elsewhere in Britain, long after the war was over. Quite detailed regulations governed each type of rationing. An example is this 44-page pamphlet explaining clothes rationing which the government distributed to the population at large.

Prefabricated homes. The huge quantity of housing damaged or destroyed in the war called for a design solution. Prefabs were quick-to-erect homes which were set up on empty sites throughout the country. Prefabs became a familiar site in postwar Thurrock and many who lived in them found their bungalow pattern layout with all facilities on one level more convenient than the homes they had lost.

Demolished in 1950 the Dutch House in High Street, Grays, had been the Grays Co-operative Society's first shop premises. In the 1950s a few of the old-style terrace and corner shops, located in what had been private houses, still remained.

Grays High Street shopping area near the end of New Road and the parish church – a typical shopping scene of the late 1940s and '50s. Most food shops in the area were still small units. Most travelled to do the shopping on foot or by bike, or by public transport for those who lived further away.

This Grays Co-op self-service shop in the late 1950s was the first sign of a trend towards the American style of shopping which has led to supermarkets and shopping malls, ideas that no one in Thurrock in the first three decades of the century would have dreamed of in the local context.

Seeing off the last passenger train on a unique light railway in 1952. The track was later to be converted to standard gauge to handle the Mobil Oil Company's freight traffic.

The demolition of Belhus House in progress, 1957. This was the grand finale to centuries of occupation of this site. In the twentieth century the house suffered the usual problems of old houses including rat-infestation.

The Knight of Aveley, designed by Whitbread's staff architect, was the first new public house to be opened on the new postwar giant estate built across the former fields in the old Aveley farming district of north-west Thurrock. It started serving customers on 22 July 1955. The name of the house was taken from a 600-year-old brass of Radulphus de Knevynton, a Crusader Knight of the fourteenth century, in the local church. The armour and chain mail worn at the time were of Flemish origin.

Above the flood water the smoke of industry at Thurrock Chalk and Whiting Company still belches out.

PUMPS GET RID OF 100 TONS OF WATER HOURLY

INSURANCE

The "Gazette" understands that many people who have suffered in the disaster are insured, and if their insurance is against "storm, flooding and tempest," or they have a comprehensive policy, they are covered in a disaster of this kind, but an ordinary policy would not cover them.

As far as television sets are concerned, it is understood that they also should be covered by a comprehensive policy.

STRANDED PIGS CARED FOR

Small pig owners at Tilbury may be reassured about the fate of their animals during the flooding at Tilbury. We understand that all but two were discovered on high patches of ground on the marshes after they had been let out and allowed take their chance early on Sunday.

OUT of the chaos which existed at Purfleet on Sunday morning has emerged—after speedy, well organised planning—an efficient system which yesterday (Thursday) afternoon had produced noticeable improvements in those areas immediately surrounding industrial sites.

An unenviable task faces the men who comprise the relief squads, for Purfleet was, in some places, over 15ft. deep in water. Van den Berghs and Jurgens, Shell and B.P. and the Esso depot were three industries worst hit by the flood. But yesterday the situation had eased to a great extent and relays of workers were travelling to and from the works by a variety of small craft.

An outstanding example of the efficient emergency control centres set up by the firms is that at the Jurgens sports pavilion; here a mobile field kitchen is working at full pressure keeping the staff and volunteers supplied with hot meals. Three huge marquees have been erected on the sports field and it is estimated that being used to take men into isolated buildings.

But all of this work has not been in vain, for with the aid of pumps which are capable of pumping away 100 tons of flood water an hour, the level has already receded by about 4ft. Another pump with the same capacity is said to be on

During the Great Flood of 1953 Thurrock was badly affected. Scenes like this one at Thurrock Chalk and Whiting's works were featured in the newspapers. The severity and suddenness of the flood took everybody by surprise (*Essex & Thurrock Gazette*, 6 February 1953).

Tilbury Library flooded.

Civic Square, Tilbury, flooded, 1953.

Fighting the floods – members of the RAF sank boats full of sandbags, which they ferried to one of the gaps in the Thames sea walls. This was the scene on 4 February 1953.

The High Street from the Police Station (now the court building), 1950s. Traffic can still use the High Street and there is no thought of Grays' eventual one-way traffic system or the Derby Road bridge for traffic to cross the railway – these are still far in the future. At this time the level crossing in the distance was still the crossing point in the centre of the town.

The High Street, looking towards the Police Station, 1950s. This was a golden age for the High Street shops. Note the parked bicycles along the kerb, left with no fears for their security. By the early 1960s, bike thefts were becoming common in Grays.

The Colourful Decades

The parade of local shops at Sockett's Heath. Up to the 1960s and '70s such local shopping facilities were highly prized and well used by customers on foot, by bike or increasingly by car. Many users on foot can be seen, some of whom are doing their main shopping here without recourse to Grays' central shopping facilities. At the end of the century the commonest way to shop is the big weekly visit to the supermarket by car. Many of these are situated on the edge of towns.

Members of the Tunnel Cement Baseball Team who swept the board in competitions in 1960. The various industries in the area provided excellent social and sporting facilities for their workers, creating a family atmosphere – so much so that the younger generation followed their parents into the same firm, building up a tradition of family involvement.

Ockendon station. The line during the 1960s ran through to Romford via Upminster, crossing the other tracks at Upminster's junction. At this time all railways fell under the shadow of the Beeching Report which recommended closure for many branch lines. An incredibly unimaginative government policy devoid of new ideas condemned many lines which might later have proved viable. Today the Ockendon branch is part of a main through service to London and there is even an extra stopping place at Chafford Hundred.

Portal of a new age, 1960. The construction of the long-delayed Dartford–Purfleet Tunnel again put Thurrock squarely on the map of road communication. This is the Kent entrance during construction, completion being scheduled for 1962, and the cost estimated at £11 million. At its deepest the tunnel is 100 ft below high water level.

Linford Pumping Station. In 1968 a very rare type of engine, a vertical turbine engine, was replaced here. Only six were known to have been made. Four were put into use in Thurrock after the First World War, one at North Stifford, two at Meeson's Lane and one at Linford, all pumping stations.

Part of the engine at Linford. Great controversy raged around the application of this type of machinery; the engines were supposed to suffer from lubrication problems and this curtailed their development. It was reported that the Linford engine had proved itself reliable, having been in constant use for a year and a half up to its final replacement.

Opening of the King George's Playing Field at Blackshots, 1961. Hugh Delargy, Thurrock's MP at this time, is second on the right. The opening heralded an era of new municipal buildings, continuing up to the 1990s.

The watery scene as the Corringham Road is flooded in 1965.

Purfleet station undergoes rebuilding in the early 1960s with a new building rising on Platform 1. The Grays and Tilbury loop was finally to cast off its steam trains and enter the era of electrification. This involved considerable engineering work and modification of lineside structures.

The level crossing near the station at Purfleet at this time. Notice the higher pedestrian overbridge crossing the line.

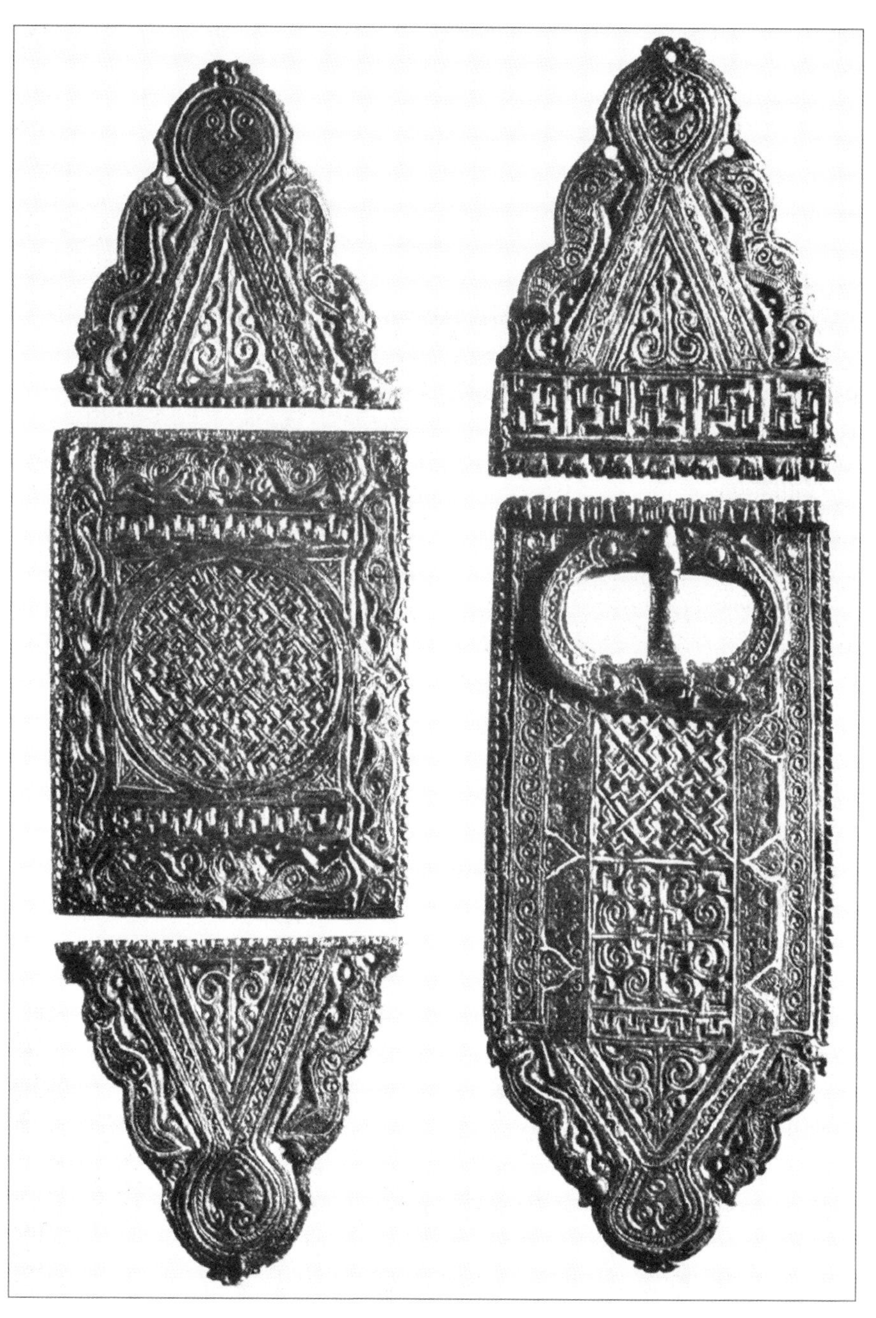

A Saxon belt discovered during the Mucking excavation. Mucking suddenly shot to fame in the 1960s. For thirteen years discovery after discovery opened up new windows on the Saxon era. Scholars from many countries avidly followed the work of M.U. Jones, leading to great advances in knowledge about this ancient people. Other discoveries in the vicinity involved the prehistoric peoples living here.

Mobil Oil Company Ltd were now operating a refinery at Coryton. Many of the staff here in the early 1960s had been ejected from Egypt at the time of the Suez Crisis when the Egyptians took control of their own oil.

A recent view of the former old High Street area. Changes and demolition in the 1960s and '70s began the process of transformation. Some of these buildings have since been rebuilt a second time. The views across the Thames are the main link with the past.

The new Grays Shopping Centre brought the main shops under cover for the first time in the 1970s, replacing old arcades such as the Ambrose Market.

The colourful centre of Grays shopping precinct as it looks in 1999.

Trolley displays give an extra dimension to the shopping centre, 1999.

The shopping mall looking towards the High Street, Grays, 1999.

The State cinema, George Street, today – still a landmark 1930s building. It has had a chequered career since the cinema's downward turn and even bingo has not rescued it. After several new beginnings it is still looking for a new role. It is a building of much merit and cries out for a sympathetic use.

Great Leaps

The striking Queen Elizabeth II Bridge, seen in the distance, heralded a further advance in communications for Thurrock. It represented a great leap of faith in design. Together with the tunnels it now forms a unit known as the Dartford Crossing. A similar view of it appeared in a successful film of the 1990s – *Four Weddings and a Funeral*. It is the longest cable-stayed bridge in Europe and was opened by the Queen on 30 October 1991.

The Lillywhite's Sports façade at Lakeside. Opening in 1990 the Lakeside shopping and entertainment complex sent shock waves rippling out over neighbouring areas. This concept, impressive in size and scope, together with a large area of parking, surpassed anything else built up to that date.

Looking up at the roof of a mall at Lakeside.

Brompton Walk, a mall with speciality shops reaching out to the lake.

Lakeside – the Food Court and lifts seen from below.

The Lake viewed from a window at Brompton Walk.

A fountain plays amid the car parking at Lakeside.

Warner Brothers Store entrance.

A major entrance into the Lakeside complex.

At the front of Lakeside the bus terminus connects the site with a large number of bus routes serving Essex, Kent and London. The area is built under the end wall of the former chalk pit. Above this a network of roads and flyovers guides the traveller towards all points of the compass, including the Channel Tunnel via the Dartford Crossing.

The approach to Chafford Hundred station. Built on the edge of the still growing Chafford Hundred housing development which is fast joining up Grays with Lakeside. A bus takes visitors to the shopping centre a few minutes away.

The Thameside Theatre and Central Library building – an important modern establishment in today's town.

Inside the Library building there are excellent displays of Thurrock's fascinating past history.

A sad memory of the 1990s is this memorial to Diana, Princess of Wales, at Orsett village.

The Foxhound, a true village pub at Orsett. Inside the proud history of the sport of quoits in the village is related. Orsett rather than Grays was once the administrative centre of the Thurrock area, and it is interesting to compare the two places at the end of the twentieth century.

Older buildings at the beginning of Stifford Clays Road, Orsett. These have still managed to retain their charm in 1999.

A quartet of shopfronts, now domestic premises. In this case uniformity delights the eye – a pre-twentieth-century attempt to provide fitting premises for the shops such as the butcher, baker, grocer and general stores is still in situ but no one could predict the way society would change its habits during the century.

Orsett Church modestly shelters behind its treescape – a rock to which tradition has clung over many centuries and still does in 1999. A footpath is signposted to the left side. At the beginning of the 1900s many villagers still used fieldpaths and back ways for most of their lives. For many there was rarely reason to venture on to the highway. . . . In 1999 the footpaths are quieter and the number of highways has increased exponentially over the century since the demise of travel by horse and the rise of the motor car.

Homes now find a place in a corner of God's acre where once the only rest was beneath the turf.

A village shop – the Orsett Stores – serving the people of the village. It marks Orsett as a fortunate place. Whereas villages at the beginning of the century in Thurrock and elsewhere were often spoilt for choice with a dozen or more establishments, in 1999 twentieth-century economics are against the survival-level of these establishments and many villages have lost every last one.

The Thamesway 'Premier' 100 bus turns the corner by the Whitmore Arms, Orsett. In 1999 the village is also fortunate to be linked with Grays, Lakeside and the county town of Chelmsford by this bus route which cuts a long swathe through Thurrock, almost bisecting it. The inn reminds us of the Whitmore family, once of Orsett Hall, who provided a Lord Lieutenant of Essex during this century (Sir Francis Whitmore).

Very close to modern development on the marshfoot of Bridge Road, Grays, these old cottages most with a front door opening straight onto the street, again connect both ends of the twentieth century. At the beginning they knew a more basic Grays. At the end they owe their survival to refurbishment techniques devised during the hundred years of progress which have made domestic life more comfortable.

The shops in Bridge have also in nearly every case completed a century of trading. Early in the century there was a boom in shopping. Local products were giving way to national branded products, the population was rising and so, slowly, were living standards, producing a demand which led to many going into shopkeeping for a living. It was very easy then – you just adapted your house slightly, providing some kind of shop window and usually turning the front room into the shop itself, without recourse to any planning regulations of importance.

Looking towards nos 1 and 3 Grove Road, Grays – just around the corner from the previous photograph. I lived at no. 1 from 1960 to 1963. At the time the premises had not been modernised in any way. As a young professional living from pay packet to pay packet with two young children and a third to be born in this house my family and I were just about surviving after paying the mortgage. In spite of this Grays was then somehow 'a different mysterious Country'. I remember lying in bed on foggy nights listening to the sound of ships' foghorns dolefully sounding out from the river and imagining myself involved in some kind of sea romance, knowing that Conrad the great novelist had lived at Stanford-le-Hope, not far away.

In 1999 the sun and shadow in Modern Clarence Road, Grays, somehow recreates the mystery and space of a past Grays. Full marks to the planners and architects.

Tilbury Riverside Station exterior from the river. This enterprising earlier 'giant leap' of the twentieth century was closed down in 1990. It had been built as an act of faith by the railway company to provide for the large number of passengers embarking on the big ocean liners connecting with the floating dock.

Interior of Tilbury Riverside station. As well as emigants to Australia and passengers on the big liners of the 1930s onwards the station had also shared in the excitement of wartime troop embarkations involving millions of soldiers. The *Windrush* and other immigrants from the West Indies also came through after the war. From a peacetime peak of a million passengers a year the numbers descended to 200 a day at the end. A replacement bus service served the ferry passengers and other visitors to this Thameside spot.

This 1995 obelisk by the Post Office in George Street is one of several imaginative pieces of public sculpture placed at key points in Grays. It was designed by Trupti Patel and has the title 'Essentials'.

A view of the 'Turoc' windvane sculpture, created by Jon Mills in 1995, and the far end of Clarence Road with its Victorian housing. The wording below the windvane supplies a poetic gloss on the Saxon word after which the town is named.

At the end of the century the railway crossing in the High Street still bars the way across the track in the same way as it did a hundred years before.

A familiar theme of waiting patiently known to all generations of Thurrock residents over the century. It has almost become an ancient ceremony – a punctuation point in the daily round where people muse on their own affairs.

When the shopfronts were built over the houses' gardens earlier in the century all the houses disappeared from view. This is the only one that remains visible today at first floor level.

On the corner of London Road, facing Quarry Hill, Commercial Buildings of 1895 has stood all century watching the tide of human affairs as well as the flow of traffic. The patterns, conceits and frills on its brickwork are still entertaining in 1999.

Yesterday and today – looking up from the Lion chalk pit towards the library and Thameside Theatre building. The disused pit is a reminder of the thriving past industry in chalk.

Standing at the corner of Cart Lane we glimpse the modern building housing the excellent theatre and library. In the same building on the first floor and with some exhibits on the ground floor is the exciting museum throwing light on Thurrock's varied history. The museum staff are real enthusiasts, busily recording every aspect of Thurrock's history.

Cart Lane from Clarence Road. This old route is a survivor of the passage taken by the chalk wagons rolling up from the pit and down to the quays on the riverside to be transshipped. Further access is now barred by recent building but this remnant is worth keeping as it is.

A very recent addition to the changing town of the last few decades of the century are the new council offices seen from the open space by the station where disused shops and warehouses stood until the 1970s. The offices are actually in New Road, once a busy shopping street at the High Street end, but now no more. This century has certainly seen some changes. Who could have foreseen those of the last few decades which have made over Grays and its surroundings anew?

Bruce's Wharf development, 1999. Even as this book is being prepared new housing is still springing up in the old riverside wharf area. Domestic pursuits now take place where once the sailing barges rode at anchor and old ships were dismantled.

Acknowledgements and Picture Credits

Thurrock Museum Service (Jonathan Catton and Terry Carney); Thurrock Libraries (Vic Tucker, Local Studies); *Thurrock Gazette*; Keith Langridge, whose photographs of modern Thurrock are a skilful and important record of the area; Thurrock Lakeside; Thurrock Council.

The 'manual instruction room' at Palmer's School, Grays, in the early 1900s.

Homestyle
FADS
SALE
GRANADA